First 100
THINGS THAT GO

On the farm

revolving
reel

combine harveste

cab

small
tractor

cab

mirror

big wheel

tire

In the air

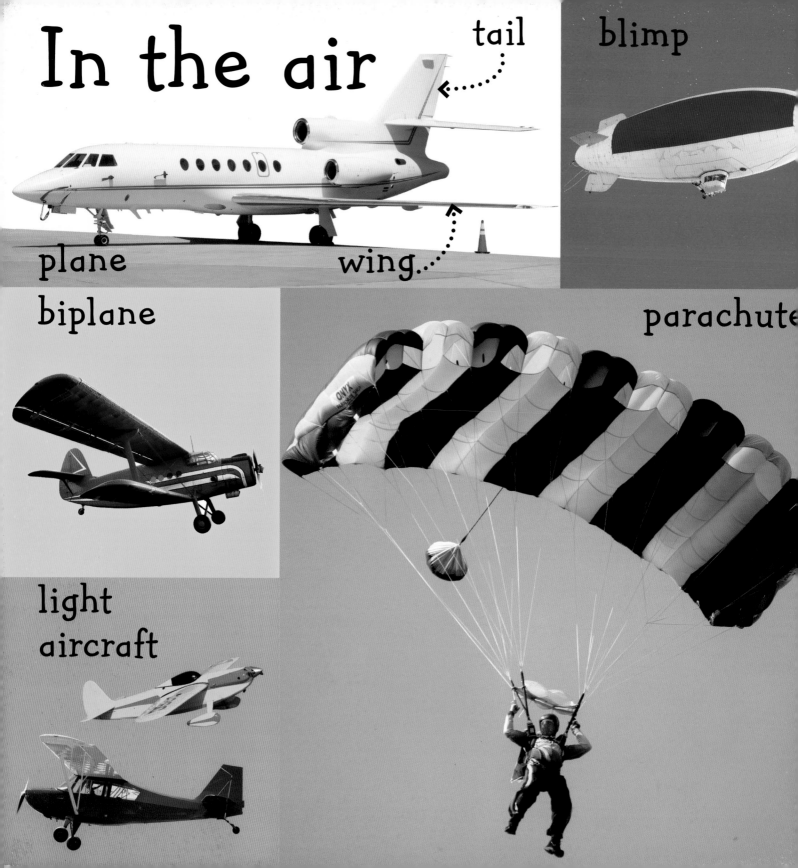

tail

blimp

plane

wing

biplane

parachute

light aircraft

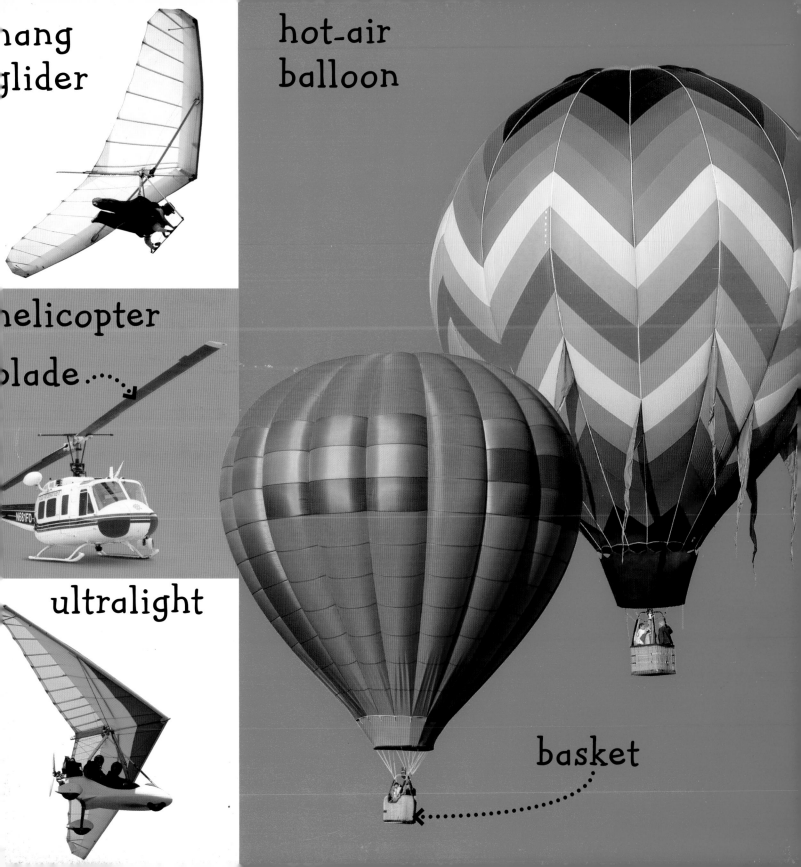

hang glider

hot-air balloon

helicopter

blade

ultralight

basket

Let's build!

backhoe loader

work lights

bucket

bulldozer

blade

dump truck

cab

fender

wheel loader

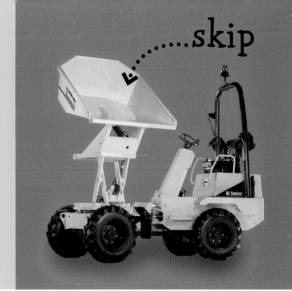 ......skip

oader

excavator

tracks

dumper

Cars

exhaust

side mirror

4x4

headlight

dune buggy

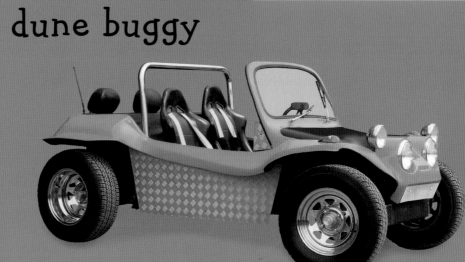

fender

hood

sports car

wheel

windshield

convertible

Trucks

dump truck

windshield

garbage truck

skip

cement truck ...... **mixer**

car carrier

side mirror

wipers

grille

Big rigs

tractor
unit

tanker

exhaust

cab

grille

wheel

headlight

sleeping cabin

trailer

Emergency

police car

police bike

motorcycle

back box

engine

police horse

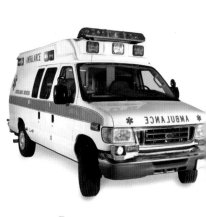

ambulance

police van

fire truck

rescue
helicopter

surveillance unit

police
boat

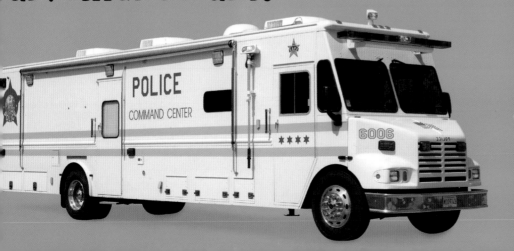

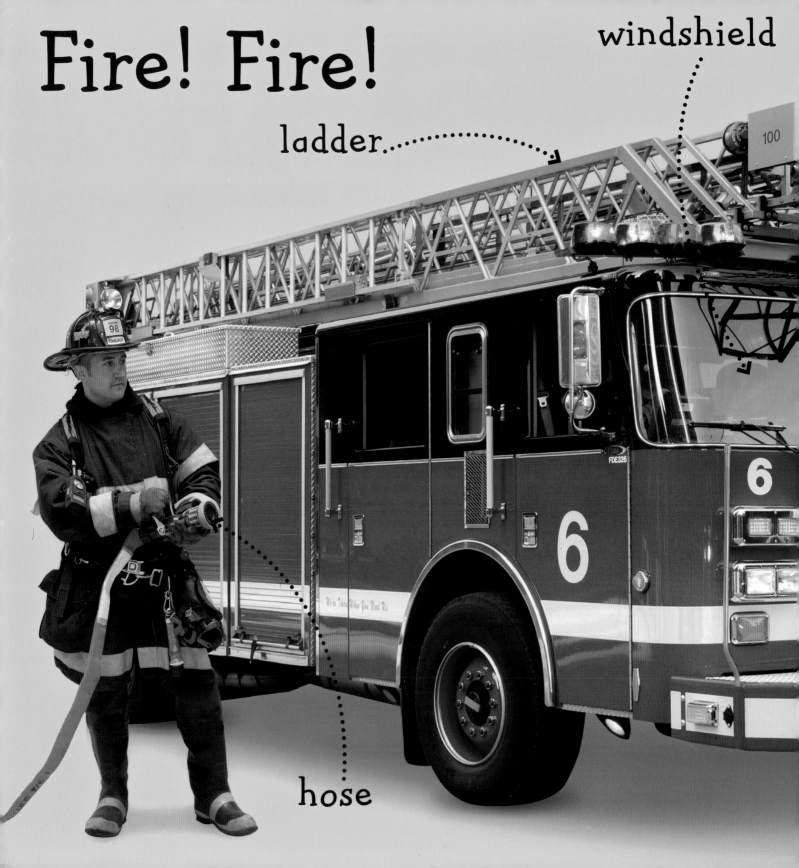

Fire! Fire!

windshield

ladder..........................

hose

lockers

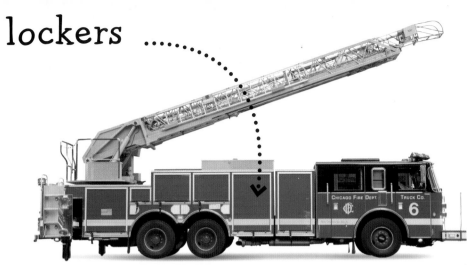

wipers

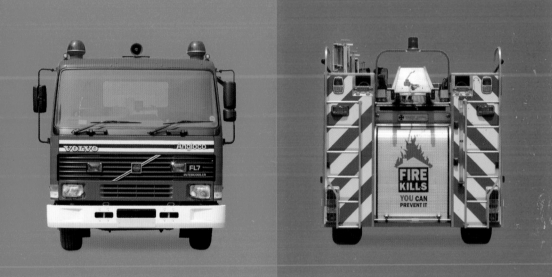

lights

fender

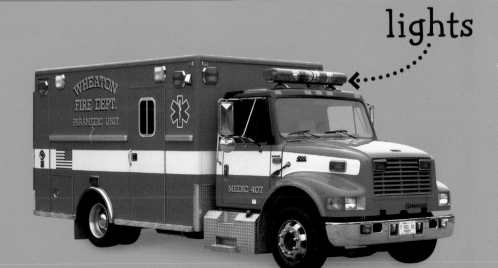

At sea

motorboat

windsurfer

sail

jet ski

boar

rubber tube

cruise ship

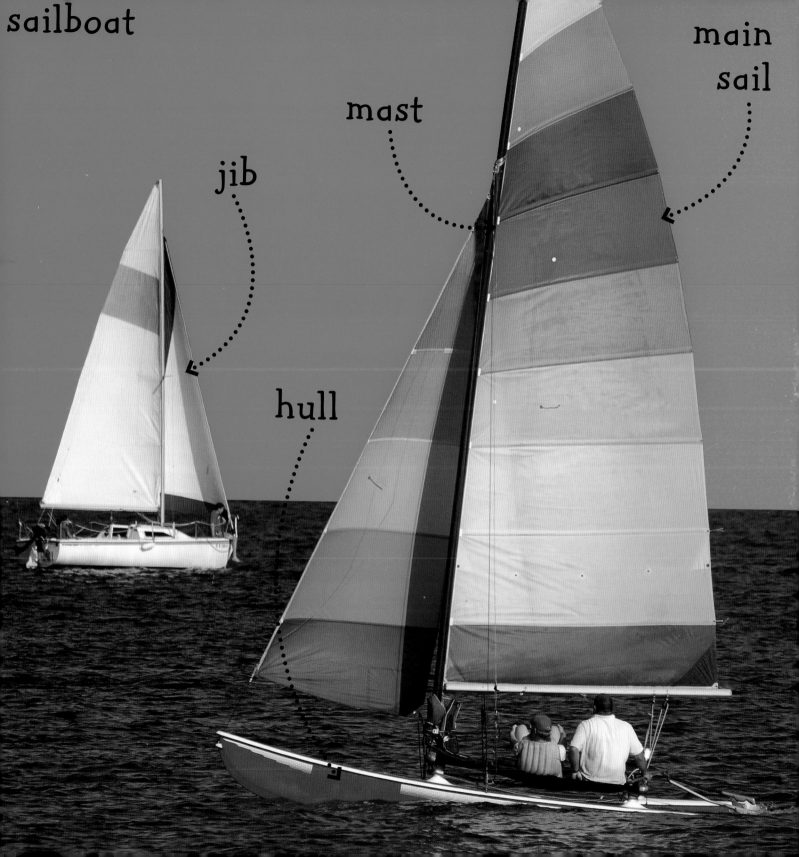

sailboat

jib

mast

main sail

hull

In the snow

snowboard

cable car

sled

skis

ski lift

ight

snowmobile

In the city

taxicabs

double-decker bus

cable car

bicycle

monorail

scooter

tram

delivery van

school bus

train